604

ABRAHAM *Lincoln*

Our PRESIDENTS

ABRAHAM *Lincoln*

OUR SIXTEENTH PRESIDENT

By Sarah Bowler

SPIRIT
of America®

The Child's World®
Chanhassen, Minnesota

ABRAHAM *Lincoln*

Published in the United States of America by The Child's World®
PO Box 326 • Chanhassen, MN 55317-0326 • 800-599-READ • www.childsworld.com

Acknowledgments
The Creative Spark: Mary Francis-DeMarois, Project Director; Elizabeth Sirimarco Budd, Series Editor;
Robert Court, Design and Art Direction; Janine Graham, Page Layout; Jennifer Moyers, Production

The Child's World®: Mary Berendes, Publishing Director; Red Line Editorial, Fact Research;
Cindy Klingel, Curriculum Advisor; Robert Noyed, Historical Advisor

Photos
Cover: White House Collection, courtesy White House Historical Association; ©Bettmann/CORBIS:
35; Chicago Historical Society: 34 (P&S-1971.0177; Artist: Alonzo Chappel); ©Corbis: 10; ©Francis
G. Mayer/CORBIS: 20; Illinois State Historical Library: 13, 19, 21, 22, 24, 25; Kevin Davidson: 26;
Library of Congress: 6, 9, 11, 12, 14, 15, 16, 27, 28, 29, 32, 33, 34 (bottom left); Courtesy of the
Lincoln Boyhood National Memorial: 7; National Archives: 31

Library of Congress Cataloging-in-Publication Data
Bowler, Sarah, 1949–
    Abraham Lincoln : our sixteenth president / by Sarah Bowler.
        p. cm.
    Includes bibliographical references and index.
    ISBN 1-56766-853-4 (lib. bdg. : alk. paper)
    1. Lincoln, Abraham, 1809–1865—Juvenile literature. 2. Presidents—United States—Biography—
Juvenile literature. [1. Lincoln, Abraham, 1809–1865. 2. Presidents.]   I. Title.
    E457.905 .B63 2001
    973.7'092—dc21

                                                                        00-010570

14   24   34

Contents

Chapter ONE

A Frontier Childhood

Many Americans believe Abraham Lincoln was the country's finest president. He is credited with saving the Union and helping to free the slaves.

WHEN HE WAS SIX YEARS OLD, ABRAHAM Lincoln walked two miles to start school in a dark log cabin. Teachers were scarce and often moved, so Abraham didn't get to go to school very much. In fact, he later said that his formal education added up to less than a year altogether! But he never stopped learning. For every new challenge, Abraham Lincoln taught himself what he needed to know, even when he became president.

The boy who would one day lead the nation spent his childhood on the **frontier** of the United States. He was born on February 12, 1809, near Hodgenville, Kentucky. His home was a rough cabin with a dirt floor. A couple of years later, the Lincoln family moved to Knob Creek, Kentucky. Abraham helped

his father farm the land. He carried water and collected firewood for his mother.

When Abraham was seven years old, the family decided to go north to Indiana, which was about to become the 19th state. They packed all their belongings on two horses, crossed the Ohio River on a **ferry,** and traveled nearly 100 miles through the wilderness to the land where they would build a new home. The forest was so dense that they had to use a wagon with runners on it, like a sleigh, to cross the thick underbrush. Then they spent

Abraham Lincoln's boyhood home is located at the Lincoln Boyhood National Memorial, near Little Pigeon Creek, Indiana.

▶ Lincoln hated the nickname "Abe." People who knew him well never called him by that name.

▶ When Lincoln was a child, young boys on the frontier wore only long, homespun shirts that came down below their knees. Their first pair of pants, often worn when boys were seven or eight years old, was usually made of buckskin.

▶ Although men and boys on the frontier hunted as a way of life, Lincoln was so upset after shooting a turkey that he never again shot at a living thing.

a bitterly cold winter in a three-sided shelter made of logs. They kept a fire burning at the open end of the shelter to provide warmth and to keep wild animals away. When spring finally arrived, Abraham helped to build their new cabin and clear the land for growing crops.

About two years later, Abraham's mother died. His sister, who was just 11 years old, tried to take over the cooking, cleaning, mending, and washing. But she was too young to handle the work alone. Their father went back to Kentucky for a short time, hoping to find a new wife. There he met a **widow** named Sarah Bush Johnston. When they returned to Indiana, Sarah set to work at once, cleaning up the rundown cabin and ragged children.

Abraham loved his stepmother. Along with a wagonload of good furniture, she brought books that she encouraged him to read. She sent the children off to a school nine miles away. When one school closed, she tried to find another. Most frontier people were too busy with the hard work of surviving to make time for education, but Abraham's stepmother knew that he was special. She helped him learn as much as

he could. One of his cousins later remembered that from the time Abraham was 12
years old, he almost always had a book in
his hand or pocket. When he was plowing
a field, he read while the horse rested at the
end of a row. At lunch, Abraham read while
he ate. When he wasn't working, he might
walk as far as 20 miles to borrow a book!

By the time he was 16, Abraham was six
feet tall, a good wrestler, and a fast runner. He
was strong and lean, and his father often hired

*Abraham often studied by
firelight after working on
his family's farm all day.
Although he couldn't
always attend school, he
worked hard to learn as
much as he could.*

At 19 years old, Abraham Lincoln traveled down the Ohio and Mississippi Rivers to New Orleans. He built a flatboat for the voyage that measured 65 feet long and 16 feet wide.

him out to work on nearby farms. Abraham enjoyed walking around the countryside, his axe on his shoulder. He often stopped to talk and joke with people, who gathered around to hear one of his stories. He became known as a funny and entertaining storyteller. Sometimes he would stand on a tree trunk and give speeches, imitating the **politicians** who visited the area.

When Abraham was 19, a man hired him to take a flatboat loaded with cargo 1,200 miles down the Ohio and Mississippi rivers to New Orleans. There he saw a busy harbor with tall sailing ships. He saw bustling city streets full of sailors from many countries. He saw slave auctions where black people were sold like cattle. It was Abraham's first look at the world beyond his own community.

10

ABRAHAM LINCOLN ONCE SAID HIS EDUCATION WAS "BY LITTLES," MEANING he went to school a little bit at a time. When he was a boy, Kentucky had no **public education.** Parents paid teachers with food, clothing, or money. Teachers often did not stay in one school for long. The first school Abraham went to was called a "blab school." It was a log cabin with one log left out of a wall to let the light in. The students had to say their lessons out loud, or "blab," so that the teacher knew they were working. The teacher stood in front, ready to punish anyone who was not "blabbing."

In those days, most schools didn't have many books, and there was very little paper. Students would do their schoolwork on whatever they could find. Lincoln was said to have written his math problems on a board or the back of a shovel with a piece of burned wood from the fireplace. Then he scraped them off with a knife when he was finished so he could do the next problem. Children often made their own arithmetic books. Some of the pages of Lincoln's book still exist today, including the one shown here.

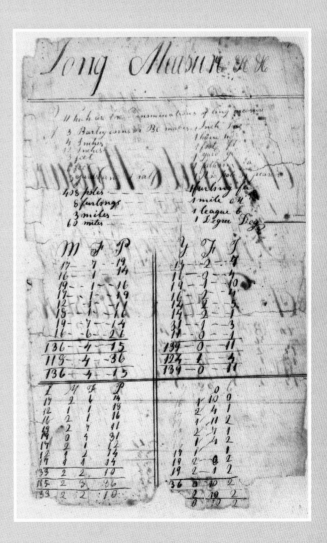

Chapter Two

Law and Politics

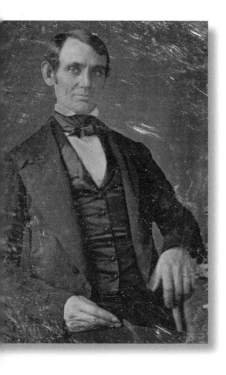

This is the first known photograph of Abraham Lincoln. It was taken in 1846, when he was 37 years old.

WHEN LINCOLN RETURNED HOME FROM NEW Orleans, he helped his family move once more, this time to Illinois. Then, at the age of 22, he was ready to set out on his own. Lincoln moved to the village of New Salem, Illinois. He got a job working in a store and made new friends easily. He joined the town's **debating** society, where he learned better grammar. In 1832, Lincoln decided to run for the **state legislature.** He talked to his neighbors and made speeches, using the public speaking skills he had developed telling stories as a teenager. Lincoln didn't win, but most of the people in his **precinct** voted for him.

Lincoln went back to storekeeping, this time as a part owner of a general store.

The store failed and left Lincoln with a huge debt of $1,100. He promised to pay it all back to the bank. He split fence rails and worked on farms. He also became the New Salem postmaster, where he enjoyed reading the newspapers that came in the mail. It would take him 15 years to repay the debt, but he would earn a reputation for honesty.

In 1834, at age 25, Lincoln again ran for the state legislature. This time he won. He bought his first suit and traveled to the state capital in a stagecoach. Then he won three more two-year **terms.** Lincoln was a good debater, and he did well in the legislature.

After he lost the election for Illinois state legislature in 1832, Lincoln became part owner of this general store in New Salem.

13

To pay back the debt from his failed store, Lincoln had to work very hard. He split logs to make rail fences, worked on farms, and even became postmaster of New Salem. Lincoln's hard work earned respect from the townspeople.

Interesting Facts

▶ When he was 23, Lincoln enlisted in a local militia (volunteer army) formed to fight Native Americans in the area. He was pleased when his friends and neighbors elected him as their captain. They never fought any Native Americans, and Lincoln later joked that he survived "a good many bloody battles with mosquitoes."

It was there that he made his first public statement on slavery, saying that it was unjust and a problem for the country.

Legislators made three dollars a day, and only during the months when the legislature was in **session.** Lincoln had to find another job. He thought of becoming a lawyer but worried about his lack of education. Finally, he decided to try. At the time, people could study law by themselves or with the help of a lawyer. They

14

were not required to go to college. Lincoln borrowed law books and studied them on his own for nearly three years. When he passed his law exams, he moved to Springfield, Illinois, on a borrowed horse with just seven dollars in his pocket. There he took a job at a law firm.

Lincoln took all kinds of **cases,** from small disputes to big trials in the Illinois **Supreme Court.** For six months of the year, he traveled with a judge and other lawyers to try cases in small towns that didn't have courts. As always, Lincoln enjoyed the chance to meet and talk to people. He became well known throughout Illinois.

Abraham Lincoln studied hard to become a lawyer. At the time, many lawyers were self-taught because few people could afford to go to college. It took three years of study, but Lincoln finally became a lawyer.

After Lincoln moved to Springfield, he met a lively young woman named Mary Todd, the daughter of a banker. Lincoln and Mary were married in 1842. Soon they bought a house where they would live for the next 17 years. Their first son, Robert, was just a baby when they moved there.

Over the years, three more sons—Edward, William, and Thomas, were born in that house. The family lived comfortably and usually had a servant to help with the housework. But Lincoln often cared for his own horse and milked the family cow.

At the end of four terms in the legislature, Lincoln wanted to become a United States congressman. He was elected to the U.S. House of Representatives in 1846, but only for one term. When he wasn't reelected, Lincoln went home to Springfield, thinking his political career was over. He worked hard in his law office and went on to become a very rich lawyer.

Lincoln and Mary Todd had much in common. They were both interested in politics, loved poetry and writing, and hated slavery. Both were eager to achieve success in life, too. This portrait of Mary Todd Lincoln is from 1846, after the Lincolns had been married for four years.

Five years later, Lincoln got involved in **politics** again. The nation was involved in a serious debate about whether to allow slavery in any new states that joined the **Union.** In 1820, a law called the Missouri Compromise had made it illegal to have slaves in any state north of a specific **latitude.** The people who supported this law hoped that if slavery could be limited, it would eventually end.

But then a law said that all new **territories** should decide for themselves if they wanted slavery. It was called the Kansas-Nebraska Act of 1854. Lincoln believed that slavery should not be allowed to spread. In 1856, he joined a **political party,** the anti-slavery **Republican Party.**

In 1858, Lincoln ran for the United States Senate against Stephen A. Douglas. He challenged Douglas to a series of debates, known as the Lincoln-Douglas debates. Reporters from as far away as New York and Boston wrote about these events for their newspapers. Lincoln lost the election, but the **campaign** made him famous around the country.

When the Republican National **Convention** met in 1860, the members of the party **nominated** Abraham Lincoln to run for president. Unlike today, presidential candidates at that time felt that it was undignified to campaign for themselves. Lincoln stayed quietly at home in Springfield while his supporters worked for him. Lincoln won the election, with nearly all of his votes coming from the Northern states.

▶ Lincoln and his law partner kept a messy office. Lincoln often couldn't find the papers he needed. He solved the problem by keeping important papers tucked inside his tall silk hat.

▶ When traveling as a lawyer, Lincoln rode a horse named Old Buck from town to town and slept in poor country inns. Sometimes he even had to share a bed with one of the other lawyers.

▶ When Lincoln was running for president, an 11-year-old girl wrote to him saying that he would look better in "whiskers" because his face was so thin. He took her advice and usually had a beard after that.

WHEN LINCOLN HEARD THAT SENATOR STEPHEN DOUGLAS OF ILLINOIS had proposed the Kansas-Nebraska bill in the U.S. Senate, he was worried that the Southern slave states were gaining too much power in the country. The South's money came mostly from **plantations,** which depended on slaves to grow and harvest the crops. The plantation owners could buy slaves, house and feed them cheaply, and have free labor. Slavery was an important part of the South's **economy.** Lincoln worried that if slavery were allowed to spread, it might one day exist in all the states, old and new, North and South.

Lincoln decided to run for the Senate against Stephen Douglas. To start his campaign, Lincoln made a passionate speech against the Kansas-Nebraska bill, saying, "A house divided against itself cannot stand. I believe this government cannot endure, permanently half slave and half free.... It will become all one thing, or all the other."

Lincoln challenged Douglas to a series of debates to be held in seven Illinois towns. There was great excitement in each town, as thousands of people came from miles around to hear the two men speak. Bands played, cannons fired, and the towns were decorated with colorful banners and flags. Newspaper reporters followed the debates, sending stories and copies of the candidates' speeches to newspapers in eastern cities such as Boston and New York.

18

The candidates could hardly have been more different. Douglas was a short man, just five feet, four inches tall. Lincoln was a full foot taller. The reporters called them "The Little Giant" and "Long Abe." Douglas wore expensive clothing and fine, ruffled shirts, while Lincoln wore a plain suit that was often wrinkled. Douglas argued that the nation could survive, half slave and half free, if each state had the right to decide for itself about slavery. Lincoln said that slavery was wrong, an evil to the whole country.

Lincoln lost the election, but it made him famous all over the nation. He was back in politics, and he was a more powerful speaker than ever because he cared deeply about the issue of slavery.

Chapter THREE

The Civil War

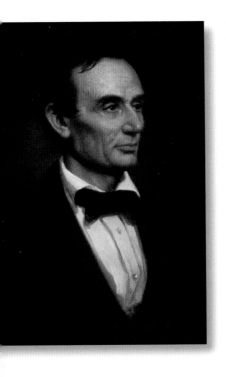

Lincoln took the oath of office on March 4, 1861, becoming the nation's 16th president. He entered office during one of the most difficult periods of American history.

LINCOLN'S PROBLEMS BEGAN BEFORE HE EVER got to Washington. Southern states were afraid that he would try to take away their right to own slaves. After Lincoln won the election, South Carolina immediately **seceded** from the Union. Then five more Southern states followed. They declared they were no longer part of the United States and wrote their own **constitution.** They established a new country called the **Confederate** States of America and elected Jefferson Davis as their president.

It was under these serious circumstances that Lincoln went to Washington to take office in March of 1861. In his **inaugural address,** he urged the Southern states not to start a war, saying they had no right "to

destroy the government, while I shall have the most solemn one to **preserve,** protect, and defend it."

A month later, his words were tested. Confederate troops had surrounded Fort Sumter in the harbor of Charleston, South Carolina. They refused to allow Union ships to get through with **provisions.** When Lincoln sent a supply ship to the soldiers at Fort Sumter, Confederate troops opened fire on the fort. The American Civil War had begun.

President Lincoln responded quickly. He declared war and asked for 75,000 volunteers to join the army. Some people believed that the United States Constitution gave these

Lincoln's inauguration took place in front of the Capitol. At the time, builders were still constructing the majestic new dome that would soon be a symbol of national pride.

21

Fort Sumter was located off the coast of Charleston, South Carolina. Before the Civil War began, it was running short of supplies. The U.S. government needed to restock its provisions or shut it down. President Lincoln decided the South would consider it a sign of weakness if he closed the fort, so he decided to send supplies and soldiers. The Confederates believed this was an act of war. They attacked Fort Sumter on April 12, 1861, and the American Civil War began.

powers to Congress, not to the president. But Lincoln believed that his Constitutional duty "to hold, occupy, and possess what belongs to the federal government" gave him the responsibility to preserve the Union. For him, the most important reason for fighting the war was to prove that a democracy like the United States could work. A democracy is a country in which the government is run by the people who live there. Lincoln wanted to prove that the Union wouldn't fall apart when there were serious disagreements among its people.

Most Northerners thought that the war would be over quickly. The North had more than twice as many people as the South. It also had factories to produce weapons and railroads to transport troops. But the South had most of the country's best generals. Most battles took place in the South, so they also had the advantage of fighting in their own territory, on land they knew well.

The first battle took place on July 21 at Bull Run, about 25 miles southwest of Washington, D.C. People drove to the battlefield in carriages. Some even took picnic lunches to eat while they watched the battle! After a few hours of fighting, the Union troops fled back to Washington. People now realized that the war was much more serious than a day's entertainment.

Lincoln didn't know much about fighting a war. But he did the same thing he always did when he wanted to achieve a goal: He read books to learn more about the subject. During the war, Lincoln helped Northern generals plan many of the battles. Sometimes he went to visit the troops. The Union had a three-part plan for winning the war. First, Lincoln

▶ At his inauguration, Lincoln looked around for a place to put his hat before he started to speak. His old rival, Stephen Douglas, stepped up and held it for him while he delivered his inaugural address.

▶ After Lincoln was elected president, he planned to take a train through major cities and speak with crowds along the way to the capital city. His plans changed when he heard there was a plot to murder him. His advisors talked him into changing his schedule, wearing a disguise, and sneaking into Washington in the middle of the night.

Lincoln visited the site where soldiers were fighting the Battle of Antietam during September and October of 1862. Lincoln took an active role in the war. He helped Union generals plan their battles and visited the troops.

Interesting Facts

▸ Early in the war, Union armies used hot air balloons to see where Confederate troops were. From an altitude of 300 feet, the balloons allowed Union soldiers to see for more than 15 miles.

▸ Many of the soldiers who fought in the Civil War were very young. About 100,000 of them were 15 years old or younger.

ordered a **blockade** of the Southern ports. This would keep the Confederacy from traveling at sea to get supplies or sell its crops. Second, the Union would invade the South and divide it into sections. The last part of the plan was to attack Richmond, Virginia, the new capital of the Confederacy.

At first, the Confederacy won most of the battles. The North did not have any military leaders that compared with the Southern generals Robert E. Lee and Thomas "Stonewall" Jackson. General George McClellan, the commander of the Union armies, was good at organizing, but he was afraid to use his army in battle. There were some victories

24

in Tennessee for the Union, but many thousands of men on both sides were killed in bloody battles. Union armies could not capture Richmond. Meanwhile, Lincoln had other tasks. Every day people lined up to see him and ask for favors. He patiently listened to all of them.

Lincoln also used these meetings with people, along with White House receptions, to find out what people thought of his **policies.** He knew he had to get people to support the Union armies. He found that many people were willing to fight to preserve the Union, but they would not fight to end slavery. Others felt that ending slavery should be the highest goal of the Civil War. Knowing how people felt helped Lincoln figure out the best time to announce new policies to the public.

The states between the North and the South, called the border states, had not joined the Confederacy. These included Kentucky, Missouri, Delaware, and Maryland. Although they were part of the Union, the

Among the many people who came to visit President Lincoln at the White House was a former slave named Sojourner Truth, who fought fiercely against slavery. After her visit, Truth said, "I am proud to say that I never was treated with more kindness and cordiality than I was by the great and good man Abraham Lincoln."

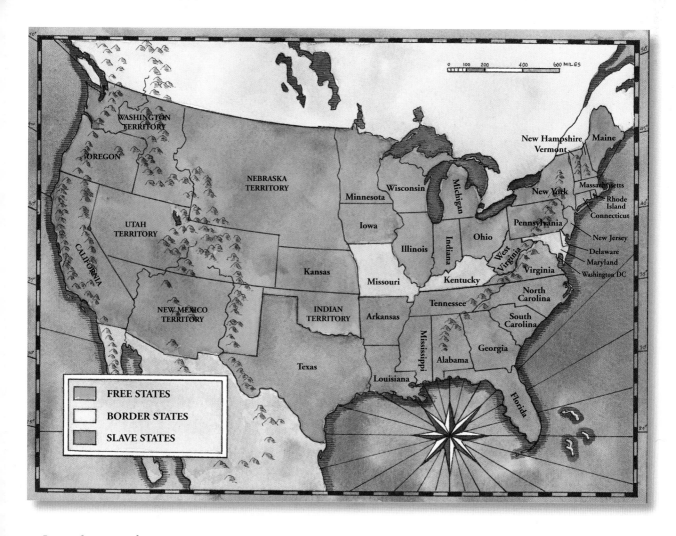

The map includes the following labels:

WASHINGTON TERRITORY

OREGON

NEBRASKA TERRITORY

UTAH TERRITORY

CALIFORNIA

NEW MEXICO TERRITORY

Minnesota

Wisconsin

Michigan

New Hampshire

Vermont

Maine

New York

Massachusetts

Rhode Island

Connecticut

Pennsylvania

New Jersey

Iowa

Ohio

Delaware

Illinois

Indiana

West Virginia

Maryland

Washington DC

Kansas

Missouri

Kentucky

Virginia

INDIAN TERRITORY

Arkansas

Tennessee

North Carolina

South Carolina

Texas

Mississippi

Alabama

Georgia

Louisiana

Florida

0 100 200 400 600 MILES

FREE STATES

BORDER STATES

SLAVE STATES

In 1861, most slave states seceded from the Union to form the Confederate States of America. But four slave states decided to fight with the Union. These were called the border states because they sat on the border between the North and the South. President Lincoln and other leaders did not outlaw slavery in these states because the Union needed their support.

citizens of these states still kept slaves. Lincoln knew that if slavery were suddenly **abolished,** these states would join the Confederacy. This would make it much more difficult for the Union to win the war. President Lincoln declared many times that the purpose of the war was to preserve the Union, not to abolish slavery. This position made **abolitionists** angry, but it kept the border states from seceding.

LINCOLN HAD LITTLE TIME TO RELAX AND ENJOY HIS TIME IN THE WHITE House. Because of the Civil War, he was busy and worried much of the time. Sometimes he would take a carriage ride with his wife, and he enjoyed going to the theater when he could. Probably his greatest pleasure was playing with his two youngest sons, Willie and Tad. He wrestled with them and took them along when he visited troops near Washington, D.C. He is shown here reading with Tad.

Lincoln wanted his boys to have a lot of freedom, and they were allowed to run wild in the White House. They would slide down banisters, interrupt important meetings, and play tricks on the people who worked there. They dragged their father to see plays they put on in the attic. They held "circuses" with the many animals they kept. Tad even slept with a pet goat on his bed!

Willie died of a fever in 1862, and Lincoln was sadder than he had ever been. Mary would not go outside for several months. Tad was lonely, trailing around behind his father. Life for the Lincoln family was never the same after Willie's death.

Chapter FOUR

Victory and Freedom

In the last year of his life, President Lincoln looked older than his 56 years. The war had been difficult and stressful for him.

LATE IN 1862, PRESIDENT LINCOLN DECIDED to change his public position on slavery. Although he had always thought slavery was wrong, he now saw several reasons to make a stronger statement against it. For one thing, he knew that more people in the North were turning against slavery. He also knew that many European countries thought slavery was a horrible thing. He believed they would be more willing to support the Union if they knew it was fighting to end slavery. Also, many slaves were running away from their owners. If they were legally free, they could serve as soldiers in the Union army.

On January 1, 1863, Lincoln signed the **Emancipation** Proclamation, a **document** stating that all slaves in the rebelling states

28

were "forever free." Although he usually signed his name "A. Lincoln," on that day he wrote out his full name. "If my name ever goes into history," he said, "it will be for this act."

The Emancipation Proclamation didn't actually free any slaves. For one thing, the Union could not enforce its laws in the Confederate states because they were no longer part of the nation. Also, the Emancipation Proclamation didn't apply to the loyal border states because Lincoln did not want to risk making them angry enough to leave the Union. He repeatedly urged the border states to voluntarily free their slaves. He even promised that the U.S. government would help pay the owners for their losses. But citizens in these states did not take his advice. Lincoln was greatly disappointed. Even though the Emancipation Proclamation didn't really free the slaves, it gave new purpose to the war. It also laid the groundwork for the

The Emancipation Proclamation made many people angry. Northerners believed it did not do enough to end slavery. Southerners believed that President Lincoln had no right to tell them what to do. After all, he was no longer their president.

13th **Amendment** to the Constitution, which would end slavery in 1865.

In May of 1863, General Ulysses S. Grant's Union forces surrounded Vicksburg, Mississippi. They bombarded the Confederate Army with cannons until it surrendered on July 4. When an army surrenders, it gives up and admits defeat. With this victory, the Union had control of the Mississippi River, separating the states east of the river from those in the West. In the East, the Battle of Gettysburg in Pennsylvania left 60,000 men killed or wounded before General Lee retreated. On November 19, 1863, Lincoln was asked to speak at the commemoration of a cemetery at Gettysburg. He spoke for less than five minutes, but that speech, known as the Gettysburg Address, would be remembered all over the world as a statement of the ideals of American democracy.

In March of 1864, Lincoln put Ulysses S. Grant in charge of all the Union armies. Grant commanded the armies near Washington and sent General William T. Sherman to take command in Tennessee. By early summer, Grant had almost surrounded Richmond. The Confederacy was close to collapse.

In Tennessee, Sherman marched eastward with 100,000 Union troops and captured Atlanta, Georgia. Then he began his famous March to the Sea. As they marched to Savannah, Georgia, on the Atlantic coast, the Northern army destroyed almost everything in its path. They weakened the South still more as they burned homes, fields, and mills and drove off farm animals.

President Lincoln's popularity had gone up and down during the course of the war, but the recent Union victories helped him get reelected. By the time he started his second term early in 1865, the end of the war was in sight. In his second inaugural address, Lincoln urged people to end the war without hatred and to heal the country's wounds. He asked people "to do all which may achieve and cherish a just and lasting peace among ourselves and with all nations."

Lincoln had trouble finding a good general until he met Ulysses S. Grant. General Grant won nearly every battle he fought. Early in 1864, Lincoln put him in charge of all the Union armies. Grant's goal was not only to fight the Confederates, but to wear them out by damaging their railroads, crops, bridges, mills, factories, and everything else they needed to make war.

Abraham Lincoln and Mary Todd Lincoln invited Union generals and politicians to a reception at the White House just as the war was ending. It was the last party held there while Lincoln was president.

That spring, Grant captured the railroads that brought supplies into Richmond. On April 9, 1865, General Lee was forced to surrender at Appomattox Courthouse in Virginia. When Grant asked Lincoln what should happen to Lee's men, Lincoln said that he wanted no man punished. He said to let them keep their horses to help plant their spring crops.

The war had been very difficult for President Lincoln, but he had done everything he could to win it. He was deeply saddened by the hundreds of thousands of young men who had died on both sides. He had slept little and eaten poorly. He had rarely found time to relax. And yet, his kind and gentle nature never left him. There are few records of Lincoln speaking harshly or bitterly to anyone through all the dark years of the war.

President Lincoln was looking forward to the work of rebuilding the nation after the terrible destruction of the war. He and Mary talked about traveling to Europe after his term was over. Then they hoped to settle down to a quiet life in Springfield. But he would never do any of these things.

Just five days after Lee's surrender, the Lincolns were watching a play at Ford's Theater in Washington. John Wilkes Booth, a famous actor and bitter anti-Unionist, crept up behind Lincoln and shot him in the head. Lincoln was carried to a room across the street from the theater where he died early the next morning, on April 15, 1865.

Mary Todd Lincoln had a difficult time during her husband's presidency. She had fewer parties than first ladies before her because of the war, so some people criticized her for not inviting guests to the president's home. Others said she spent too much money on clothing and furnishings for the White House. These insults hurt Mrs. Lincoln at first. But after her son Willie died, nothing else mattered. His loss devastated her.

Abraham Lincoln died on April 15, 1865. The nation could no longer rely on his leadership to help restore the tattered Union.

Below: John Wilkes Booth was not the only man involved in the plot to kill President Lincoln. This poster offers a reward for Booth and two men who helped him, John Surrat and David Harold. Six days after this poster was issued, Booth was captured and shot in Virginia.

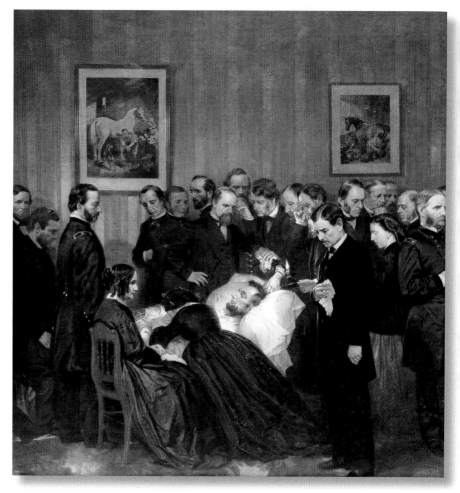

Many people think that Abraham Lincoln was America's greatest president. From his rough frontier childhood, he grew up to become a brilliant leader. Even today, his powerful speeches help us to understand and remember the values upon which the United States was created. He freed the slaves and kept the country from breaking apart. He proved to the world that democracy could work.

WHEN THE ARMIES BURIED SOME 40,000 DEAD SOLDIERS AT GETTYSBURG, they didn't stay buried. Rain uncovered thousands of the bodies, and the people of Gettysburg knew they had to do something. With the help of Northern governors, they raised money to create the National Soldiers' Cemetery on the battlefield. Then they reburied the dead.

The ceremony to dedicate the cemetery was held on November 19, 1863. Between 15,000 and 20,000 people gathered to take part in the event. The main speaker was Edward Everett, America's leading speechmaker at that time. He spoke for two hours. President Lincoln also spoke at the event. When it was his turn, he rose, put on his glasses, and took two sheets of paper from his pocket. His speech was less than five minutes long. When Lincoln returned to his seat, the audience was quiet. Many of the people were disappointed. Lincoln himself felt the speech had been a failure. Some newspapers reported that it was dull, but others said it was a work of genius.

It was, in fact, an important speech. In simple, beautiful words, Lincoln asked that people remember the ideals for which the soldiers had fought. He asked them to remember the Declaration of Independence, which says that all men are created equal. He said the soldiers who fought for this ideal did not die for nothing, but to preserve democracy. Lincoln reminded his audience that the soldiers gave their lives to prove that "government of the people, by the people, for the people, shall not perish from the earth."

1809 Abraham Lincoln is born on February 12 at Sinking Spring Farm, near what is now Hodgenville, Kentucky. His parents were Thomas Lincoln and Mary Hanks Lincoln.

1811 Lincoln moves to Knob Creek with his parents and his sister, Sarah. This is the first home he will remember.

1815 Lincoln goes to school for the first time and learns to read and write.

1816 The family moves to Indiana to start a new farm. Lincoln will remember the trip as the hardest experience of his life.

1818 Lincoln's mother dies.

1819 Thomas Lincoln marries Sarah Bush Johnston.

1828 Lincoln takes a flatboat 1,200 miles down the Ohio and Mississippi Rivers to New Orleans.

1830 Lincoln helps his family move to Illinois. He stays to help build the house and start the farm before setting off on his own.

1831 Lincoln takes another boatload of cargo to New Orleans with his cousin and stepbrother. In July, he goes to live in New Salem, Illinois.

1832 Lincoln is elected captain of a volunteer militia.

1833 Lincoln becomes the New Salem postmaster, earning about $50 a year.

1834 Lincoln is elected to the Illinois state legislature for the first time. He goes on to be reelected for three more two-year terms and serves for a total of eight years.

1837 After studying law for nearly three years, Lincoln passes his exams and is admitted into law practice on March 1.

1842 Lincoln marries Mary Todd on November 4.

1843 The Lincolns' first son, Robert Todd, is born.

1844 The Lincolns move to a house in Springfield where they go on to live for the next 17 years. It is the only house that Lincoln ever owns.

1846 The Lincolns' second son, Eddie, is born. Lincoln is elected to the United States House of Representatives. He serves a single two-year term.

1850 Eddie Lincoln dies of an illness at the age of three.

1850 The Lincolns' third son, Willie, is born.

1853 The Lincolns' fourth son, Thomas, is born. His parents call him Tad.

1854   Congress passes the Kansas-Nebraska Act, opening the spread of slavery to new territories. Lincoln, who had been losing interest in politics, neglects his law practice and speaks out against the Act.

1856   Lincoln joins the Republican Party, which opposes slavery.

1858   Lincoln wins the Republican nomination for the U.S. Senate and launches his campaign with a fiery speech against the idea of a country that is half slave and half free. In the summer, Lincoln challenges the Democratic candidate, Stephen Douglas, to a series of debates, which makes Lincoln well known around the country.

1860   Lincoln is chosen as the Republican candidate for the presidency. He is elected on November 6. In December, South Carolina announces that it is seceding from the Union and is dedicated to the preservation of slavery.

1861   Lincoln takes office on March 4. On April 12, Confederate cannons fire on Fort Sumter, and the Civil War begins. Lincoln immediately calls for 75,000 volunteers to join the Union army. The Battle of Bull Run takes place in July a few miles from Washington, D.C. Union troops under General Irwin McDowell break ranks and flee back to Washington.

1862   Willie Lincoln dies of fever in February, sending Lincoln into a deep depression. Union troops win battles at Fort Henry, Fort Donelson, and Fort Shiloh under General Ulysses S. Grant.

1863   Lincoln signs the Emancipation Proclamation, a document freeing the slaves in the Confederate states. In May, General Grant's armies take over Vicksburg, Mississippi, gaining control of the Mississippi River. Union armies win the Battle of Gettysburg in July. In November, Lincoln delivers the Gettysburg Address.

1864   General Grant takes command of all Union armies. In November, General Sherman's troops begin their March to the Sea in Georgia. They capture Atlanta and then Savannah.

1865   On January 31, the House of Representatives approves the 13th Amendment, ending slavery in the United States. Lincoln takes the oath of office on March 4 to begin his second term as president. On April 9, Confederate General Robert E. Lee surrenders at Appomattox Courthouse in Virginia. Lincoln is shot by John Wilkes Booth at Ford's Theater on April 14. He dies the next morning.

abolish (uh-BOHL-ish)
If something is abolished, it has been stopped or ended. The Southern states did not want to abolish slavery.

abolitionists (ab-uh-LISH-uh-nists)
Abolitionists were people who wanted to put an end to slavery before and during the Civil War. Abolitionists wanted President Lincoln to end slavery in all the states.

amendment (uh-MEND-ment)
An amendment is a change or addition to the Constitution or other document. The 13th Amendment outlawed slavery in the United States.

blockade (blaw-KAYD)
A blockade keeps people and supplies from moving in or out of an area. A blockade of the Southern ports caused the people of the South to lose money because they couldn't sell their crops to European markets.

campaign (kam-PAYN)
A campaign is the process of running for an election, including activities such as giving speeches or attending rallies. Lincoln's campaign in 1860 was successful, and he was elected president.

cases (KAY-sez)
Cases are matters decided by a court of law. Lawyers argue cases in court before a judge.

Confederate (kun-FED-uh-ret)
A Confederate was a person who lived in, supported, or fought for the Confederate States of America during the Civil War. The Confederates seceded from the Union.

constitution (kon-stuh-TOO-shun)
A constitution is the set of basic principles that govern a state, country, or society. The Confederates wrote their own constitution.

convention (kun-VEN-shun)
A convention is a meeting. Abraham Lincoln was nominated for president at the Republican National Convention in 1860.

debating (dih-BAY-ting)
Debating means taking part in a contest in which opponents argue for opposite sides of an issue. Lincoln was good at debating.

document (DOK-yuh-ment)
A document is a written or printed paper that gives people important information. The Emancipation Proclamation was a document written to free slaves in the South.

economy (ee-KON-uh-mee)
An economy is the way money is earned and spent by a government. The South's economy depended on slave labor to help grow crops.

**emancipation
(ee-man-seh-PAY-shun)**
Emancipation is the act of setting someone free. The Emancipation Proclamation set slaves free in the rebelling states.

ferry (FAYR-ee)
A ferry is a boat used to transport people and goods. A ferry took the Lincolns, their two horses, and all their belongings across the river.

frontier (frun-TEER)
A frontier is a region that is at the edge of or beyond settled land. In Lincoln's youth, Kentucky was part of the U.S. frontier.

**inaugural address
(ih-NAWG-yuh-rul uh-DRESS)**
An inaugural address is the speech that an elected president makes at his inauguration. An inauguration is the ceremony that takes place when a new president begins a term.

latitude (LAT-uh-tood)
Latitude is the distance of a place as measured north or south from the equator. On globes and maps, lines of latitude run east and west. The latitude of the southern border of Missouri marked the point below which slavery was legal.

nominate (NOM-uh-nayt)
If a political party nominates someone, it chooses him or her to run for a political office. Each party holds a convention to nominate a presidential candidate.

plantations (plan-TAY-shunz)
Plantations are large farms or groups of farms that grow crops such as tobacco, sugarcane, or cotton. Southern plantations depended on the labor of slaves to grow their crops.

policies (PAWL-uh-seez)
Policies are rules made to help run a government or other organization. Lincoln wanted to know what people thought of his policies.

**political party
(puh-LIT-uh-kul PAR-tee)**
A political party is a group of people who share similar ideas about how to run a government. Lincoln joined the Republican Party in 1856.

politicians (pawl-uh-TISH-unz)
Politicians are people who run for elected offices. As a child, Lincoln imitated politicians giving speeches.

politics (PAWL-uh-tiks)
Politics refers to the actions and practices of the government. Lincoln returned to politics because he did not want slavery to spread.

precinct (PRE-sinkt)
A precinct is a district of a city or a town. Most of the people in Lincoln's precinct voted for him when he ran for Illinois state legislature in 1832.

preserve (pree-ZERV)
If people preserve something, they keep it from harm or change. Lincoln wanted to preserve the Union.

provisions (pro-VIZH-unz)
Provisions are a stock of necessary items, especially food. The soldiers at Fort Sumter were running out of provisions before the Civil War began.

**public education
(PUB-lik edj-yoo-KAY-shun)**
Public education is a school system supported by the government and its taxpayers. Before there was public education on the frontier, families had to pay their children's teachers.

**Republican Party
(ree-PUB-lih-ken PAR-tee)**
The Republican Party is one of the two major U.S. political parties. President Lincoln was a Republican.

secede (suh-SEED)
If a group secedes, it separates from a larger group. South Carolina was the first state to secede from the Union.

session (SESH-un)
A session is a series of meetings of a legislative body. When Lincoln was in office the yearly session for the Illinois state legislature lasted about 100 days.

**state legislature
(STAYT LEJ-uh-slay-chur)**
A state legislature is the part of a state's government that makes laws. Lincoln was elected to the Illinois state legislature four times in a row.

**supreme court
(suh-PREEM KORT)**
A supreme court is the most powerful court in an individual state. Lincoln took cases to the Illinois Supreme Court when he worked as a lawyer.

terms (TERMZ)
Terms are the length of time politicians can keep their positions by law. In Lincoln's time, a term in the Illinois state legislature was two years.

territories (TAYR-ih-tor-eez)
Territories are lands or regions, especially lands that belong to a government. The Kansas-Nebraska Act said that all new territories should decide for themselves if they wanted slavery to be legal.

Union (YOON-yen)
The Union is another name for the United States of America. During the Civil War, the North was called the Union.

widow (WID-oh)
A widow is a woman whose husband has died. Lincoln's father married a widow named Sarah Bush Johnston.

Our PRESIDENTS

President	Birthplace	Life Dates	Term	Political Party	First Lady
George Washington	Virginia	1732–1799	1789–1797	None	Martha Dandridge Custis Washington
John Adams	Massachusetts	1735–1826	1797–1801	Federalist	Abigail Smith Adams
Thomas Jefferson	Virginia	1743–1826	1801–1809	Democratic-Republican	widower
James Madison	Virginia	1751–1836	1809–1817	Democratic-Republican	Dolley Payne Todd Madison
James Monroe	Virginia	1758–1831	1817–1825	Democratic-Republican	Elizabeth "Eliza" Kortright Monroe
John Quincy Adams	Massachusetts	1767–1848	1825–1829	Democratic-Republican	Louisa Catherine Johnson Adams
Andrew Jackson	South Carolina	1767–1845	1829–1837	Democrat	widower
Martin Van Buren	New York	1782–1862	1837–1841	Democrat	widower
William Henry Harrison	Virginia	1773–1841	1841	Whig	Anna Tuthill Symmes Harrison
John Tyler	Virginia	1790–1862	1841–1845	Whig	Letitia Christian Tyler Julia Gardiner Tyler
James Polk	North Carolina	1795–1849	1845–1849	Democrat	Sarah Childress Polk

Our PRESENTS

President	Birthplace	Life Dates	Term	Political Party	First Lady
Zachary Taylor	Virginia	1784–1850	1849–1850	Whig	Margaret Mackall Smith Taylor
Millard Fillmore	New York	1800–1874	1850–1853	Whig	Abigail Powers Fillmore
Franklin Pierce	New Hampshire	1804–1869	1853–1857	Democrat	Jane Means Appleton Pierce
James Buchanan	Pennsylvania	1791–1868	1857–1861	Democrat	never married
Abraham Lincoln	Kentucky	1809–1865	1861–1865	Republican	Mary Todd Lincoln
Andrew Johnson	North Carolina	1808–1875	1865–1869	Democrat	Eliza McCardle Johnson
Ulysses S. Grant	Ohio	1822–1885	1869–1877	Republican	Julia Dent Grant
Rutherford B. Hayes	Ohio	1822–1893	1877–1881	Republican	Lucy Ware Webb Hayes
James A. Garfield	Ohio	1831–1881	1881	Republican	Lucretia Rudolph Garfield
Chester A. Arthur	Vermont	1829–1886	1881–1885	Republican	widower
Grover Cleveland	New Jersey	1837–1908	1885–1889	Democrat	Frances Folsom Cleveland

Our PRESIDENTS

President	Birthplace	Life Dates	Term	Political Party	First Lady
Benjamin Harrison	Ohio	1833–1901	1889–1893	Republican	Caroline Lavina Scott Harrison
Grover Cleveland	New Jersey	1837–1908	1893–1897	Democrat	Frances Folsom Cleveland
William McKinley	Ohio	1843–1901	1897–1901	Republican	Ida Saxton McKinley
Theodore Roosevelt	New York	1858–1919	1901–1909	Republican	Edith Kermit Carow Roosevelt
William Howard Taft	Ohio	1857–1930	1909–1913	Republican	Helen Herron Taft
Woodrow Wilson	Virginia	1856–1924	1913–1921	Democrat	Ellen L. Axson Wilson / Edith Bolling Galt Wilson
Warren G. Harding	Ohio	1865–1923	1921–1923	Republican	Florence Kling De Wolfe Harding
Calvin Coolidge	Vermont	1872–1933	1923–1929	Republican	Grace Anna Goodhue Coolidge
Herbert Hoover	Iowa	1874–1964	1929–1933	Republican	Lou Henry Hoover
Franklin D. Roosevelt	New York	1882–1945	1933–1945	Democrat	Anna Eleanor Roosevelt Roosevelt
Harry S. Truman	Missouri	1884–1972	1945–1953	Democrat	Elizabeth "Bess" Virginia Wallace Truman

Our PRESIDENTS

President	Birthplace	Life Dates	Term	Political Party	First Lady
Dwight D. Eisenhower	Texas	1890–1969	1953–1961	Republican	Mamie Geneva Doud Eisenhower
John F. Kennedy	Massachusetts	1917–1963	1961–1963	Democrat	Jacqueline Lee Bouvier Kennedy
Lyndon Baines Johnson	Texas	1908–1973	1963–1969	Democrat	Claudia "Lady Bird" Alta Taylor Johnson
Richard M. Nixon	California	1913–1994	1969–1974	Republican	Thelma "Pat" Catherine Patricia Ryan Nixon
Gerald R. Ford	Nebraska	1913–	1974–1977	Republican	Elizabeth "Betty" Bloomer Warren Ford
James Earl Carter	Georgia	1924–	1977–1981	Democrat	Rosalynn Smith Carter
Ronald Reagan	Illinois	1911–	1981–1989	Republican	Nancy Davis Reagan
George Bush	Massachusetts	1924–	1989–1993	Republican	Barbara Pierce Bush
William J. Clinton	Arkansas	1946–	1993–2001	Democrat	Hillary Rodham Clinton
George W. Bush	Connecticut	1946–	2001–	Republican	Laura Welch Bush

Presidential FACTS

Qualifications
To run for president, a candidate must
- be at least 35 years old
- be a citizen who was born in the United States
- have lived in the United States for 14 years

Term of Office
A president's term of office is four years. No president can stay in office for more than two terms.

Election Date
The presidential election takes place every four years on the first Tuesday of November.

Inauguration Date
Presidents are inaugurated on January 20.

Oath of Office
I do solemnly swear I will faithfully execute the office of the President of the United States and will to the best of my ability preserve, protect, and defend the Constitution of the United States.

Write a Letter to the President
One of the best things about being a U.S. citizen is that Americans get to participate in their government. They can speak out if they feel government leaders aren't doing their jobs. They can also praise leaders who are going the extra mile. Do you have something you'd like the president to do? Should the president worry more about the environment and encourage people to recycle? Should the government spend more money on our schools? You can write a letter to the president to say how you feel!

1600 Pennsylvania Avenue
Washington, D.C. 20500

You can even send an e-mail to: president@whitehouse.gov

For Further INFORMATION

Internet Sites

Find more information on Lincoln, including photographs and an e-mail address to answer questions:
members.aol.com/RVSNorton/Lincoln2.html

Read quotes from Abraham Lincoln:
www.cc.columbia.edu/acis/bartleby/bartlett/422.html

Find information about the Lincoln Boyhood National Memorial:
www.nps.gov/libo

Learn more about Mary Todd Lincoln:
www.whitehouse.gov/WH/glimpse/firstladies/html/ml16.html

Find historical resources about the Civil War, including time lines, historic figures, and life stories:
americancivilwar.com
http://www.civilwarhome.com/
http://mirkwood.ucs.indiana.edu/acw/

Find a children's listing of other Civil War sites:
www.kidinfo.com/American_History/Civil_War.html

Books

Freedman, Russell. *Lincoln: A Photobiography.* New York: Houghton Mifflin, 1987.

Graham, Martin F., Richard A. Sauers, and George Skoch. *The Blue and the Gray.* Lincolnwood, IL: Publications International, 1996.

Lester, Julius. *To Be a Slave.* New York: Scholastic, 1968.

Marrin, Albert. *Commander in Chief Abraham Lincoln and the Civil War.* New York: Dutton Children's Books, 1997.

Morris, Jeffrey. *The Lincoln Way* (Great Presidential Decisions). Minneapolis, MN: Lerner Publications, 1996.

Index

48